How to design a
Chair

**DESIGN
MUSEUM**

How to design a
Chair

conran
OCTOPUS

Previous page:
The Y or Wishbone chair,
designed by Hans Wegner
in 1949, was originally
produced in teak but is
now available in a range
of colours and finishes.

CENTRE	NEWARK
CHECKED	
ZONE	BLACK
ZONE MARK / SUFFIX	749.32 WIL
LOAN PERIOD	1 MONTH

How to design a Chair

Introduction

Swan, Antelope, Ox... Bubble, Egg, Womb... Tulip, Teddy Bear, Butterfly...

The chair is an immensely suggestive form. It is one of the most anthropomorphic furniture types: it has a back, a seat and legs, sometimes arms, and occasionally elbows, knees and feet. It sits and invites sitting – even unoccupied, it has a certain human presence. In this light, *Vincent's Chair with His Pipe* (1988), the famous painting by Vincent van Gogh of a simple rush-bottomed wooden chair, can be seen as a self-portrait of the artist, or rather as a 'self-portrait as a chair', as the eminent US philosopher Arthur C Danto pointed out in *397 Chairs* (1988).

All through life, we play a game of musical chairs – moving from rockers to high chairs, school chairs to office chairs, armchairs to rockers again. We assume roles – we may become 'the Chair' of a committee or 'a Chair' (of history, for example), or we may prefer to take a back seat. From time to time we may find ourselves in the dentist's chair or other uncomfortable places.

To these associations and many others, designers of chairs have brought their own agendas. 'When we design a chair, we design a society and a city in miniature,' wrote the British architect Peter Smithson. 'The Miesian city is implicit in the Miesian chair.' A chair, as Le Corbusier pointed out, is a 'machine for sitting on', but it is evidently much more than that.

Right: *Vincent's Chair with His Pipe*, painted by Van Gogh in Arles in 1888, at a time when he was working alongside Paul Gauguin. Van Gogh painted a companion picture, *Gauguin's Armchair*, around the same time.

Below: The Teddy Bear chair (1950) by Hans Wegner (1914–2007) is so called because a critic remarked that the arms resembled bear paws reaching round to give you a hug. The wooden 'paws' are more resistant to wear and soiling than fully upholstered arms would be.

Right: The Pelican chair was designed by Finn Juhl (1912–89) in 1940, for use in his own home. Like Wegner's Teddy Bear chair, it is a reinterpretation of the classic wing chair.

Principles

When in 1970 Jonathan de Pas (1932–91), Donato D'Urbino (1935–), Paolo Lomazzi (1936–) and Carla Scolari designed the Joe chair (which takes the form of an overscaled baseball mitt), they were responding to a comment by a client who said a chair should 'fit like a glove'. The result is a chair that tells a joke. Almost 40 years earlier, the Finnish architect and designer Alvar Aalto (1898–1976) produced a three-legged stool (Model No. 60; c1932–3) that made use of the bent L-leg, a design so economical in every respect that it is virtually an archetype. Each answers a very different question about what a chair is supposed to do.

Below: The Joe chair (1970) is a design that tells a joke. Taking the form of an over-scaled baseball mitt, it makes a play on the notion that a chair should fit like a glove. The name refers to the famous New York Yankees centrefielder Joe DiMaggio.

Right: The patent drawing of the L-leg, the essential structural component of Alvar Aalto's stacking stool.

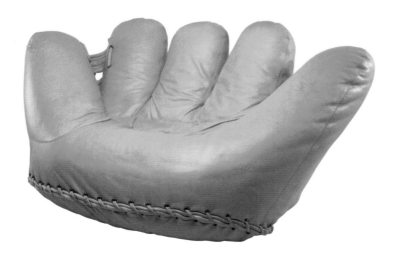

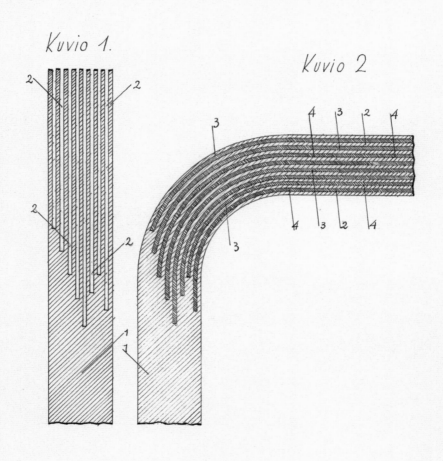

Kuvio 1.

Kuvio 2

A. Aalto.

Left: The Karuselli chair (c1965) by the Finnish designer Yrjö Kukkapuro has a contoured moulded fibreglass seat shape inspired by snow chairs the designer made with his daughter one winter.

Below: A good task chair should support the body in different postures and allow for movement to prevent back strain and other problems associated with sitting for long periods. The Aeron chair (1992) is so adjustable that it has been certified for 24-hour usage.

Function

Whatever else a chair does, or is, it must support the seated body without breaking or falling over. The bottom line is strength. The framework or support structure must be strong enough to hold together, and the seat and back strong enough to bear the weights imposed on them.

What type of support a chair provides, however, is dictated by use. A chair can be upright, incorporate arm, head or foot rests, enclose its occupant in a padded interior, recline, or respond to shifts in posture. An upright chair that can be pulled up to a table provides a comfortable posture for eating. A desk chair, in which you might sit for many hours at a time, should allow the body to move, to prevent the back strain that can result from being forced to sit in one position for too long. Easy chairs for relaxing are often reclining, so that weight shifts from the seat to the back.

Seat depth and seat height are the two most critical dimensions in chair design. A seat that is too high leaves the feet dangling and results in too much pressure on the backs of the knees. A seat that is too low can increase pressure on the bones at the base of the spine. A shallow seat pitches the weight forward, whereas one that is too deep throws it uncomfortably backward. Anthropometric measurements applied to chair design help to ensure that weight is distributed comfortably. Padding serves a similar function, by increasing the points of contact between the body and the chair.

A classic example of a chair that is a product of intense ergonomic research is the Aeron task chair, designed in 1992 by Donald T Chadwick (1936–) and Bill Stumpf (1936–2006). It comes in three different sizes to suit different body frames, and is so adjustable (forward tilt, pneumatic lift, vertical- and depth-adjusting lumbar pads, height-adjustable arms that can also pivot) that is has been certified for 24-hour use, as opposed to the usual eight. The seat and back material is a special tensile mesh that distributes weight and allows air to circulate.

A rather more ad hoc process of development went into the Karuselli chair (c1965), by the Finnish furniture designer Yrjö Kukkapuro (1933–). He had been playing with his daughter one winter, making snow chairs in the deep drifts outside his house, when he was inspired to see if he could recreate the same supportive, contoured shape in a chair seat. A year later, after a lengthy process of experimenting with chicken wire covered in canvas and dipped in plaster, he took the fibreglass prototype along to a furniture shop to gauge possible interest. Although it was before opening hours, a passer-by wandered into the shop, sat in the chair and said he would take one.

Chairs are naturally defined by their prime function, which is to serve as a place to sit. But there are many other functions they might be called on to provide. Stacking and folding chairs address the need for spacesaving and portability. The Plia chair (1969) by Giancarlo Piretti (1940–), with its transparent moulded seat and back and exceptionally shallow depth when folded or stacked, combines this type of flexibility with a pleasing reticence.

Is the chair intended for outdoor or indoor use? Public or domestic? Price, maintenance, robustness, weight are also factors for chair designers to consider. Increasingly these days, environmental considerations come the fore: is the material sustainable, recyclable, recycled? Jasper Morrison's (1959–) Monopod chair (2008) for Vitra is made out of recycled wine bottle corks upholstered in leather.

Right: The chair as functional ready-made or found object. Ron Arad's iconic Rover chair (1981) is a fusion of a scrapyard seat from a Rover 2000 mounted on a frame made of Kee Klamp scaffolding. It was produced by OneOff.

Below: How High the Moon (1986) by the Japanese designer Shiro Kuramata (1934–91) dematerializes the form of the chair to a point where it almost looks fragile and incapable of supporting the body. The chair is made of nickel-plated steel mesh and has no interior frame.

Presence

It is not surprising that many architects have been designers of chairs as well. A chair conceived for a specific context is a way of achieving unity and control, of making a statement about design intent. Arne Jacobsen (1902–71) designed furniture and fittings for many of his buildings, for example, right down to the pulls on blind cords.

Chairs not only occupy space, they serve as spatial markers. Charles Rennie Mackintosh's (1868–1928) attenuated chairs, such as the ladder-back designed for the bedroom at Hill House (1902), and the Ingram high-back chair (1900) designed for a Glasgow tearoom, are supreme examples of spatial markers, their vertical emphasis a form of architectural detail, or in the case of the Ingram chair forming a palisade or intimate enclosure around the focus of a table.

Chairs also *contain* space. Designs such as Eero Aarnio's (1932–) Ball chair (1963), a fibreglass ball lined with upholstery, are spaces within spaces, where the occupant is cocooned in a world of their own. Aarnio's own version of the chair included a telephone; others

Below: The Ingram high-back chair (1900), designed by the architect Charles Rennie Mackintosh for a Glasgow tearoom, is a prime example of the chair as spatial marker. Ranged round a table, the chairs create a private enclosure.

Right: The Bubble chair (1968) by Finnish designer Eero Aarnio used similar technology to that involved in the production of domed acrylic skylights. The girls seated in this pair of chairs are the designer's daughters.

have incorporated speakers. Business-class airline seats, which multi-task as beds, dining areas and entertainment zones, are similarly encompassing. And, of course, chairs are personal territory: 'Who's been sitting in *my* chair?'

Another way in which chairs make their presence known is through the expression of a manifesto, an agenda or an artistic or political stance. The Favela chair (2003), by the Brazilian designers Humberto (1953–) and Fernando Campana (1961–), is a brittle commentary on the rudimentary shelters that proliferate around the fringes of Rio de Janeiro, cobbled together from whatever is to hand. The chair consists of scraps of wood, haphazardly glued and nailed in place, piece by piece.

Wit and the jolt of the unexpected can also come into play. Achille (1918–2002) and Pier Giacomo (1913–68) Castiglioni's Mezzandro stool (1954–7) joined a tractor seat to a bent-metal support. Ron Arad's (1951–) ready-made Rover chair (1981) married a scrap car seat with Kee Klamp scaffolding: the chair as found object. The point of departure for Vico Magistretti's (1920–2006) Sinbad chair (1982) was a horse blanket he found in a London shop and which he used to drape over a metal frame to form the seat cover.

Right and below: The Favela chair (2003), designed by the Brazilian Campana brothers, creates a kind of richness and elaboration through the assembly of 'poor' materials, such as scraps of pinewood. The brothers are inspired by Brazilian street life and culture, and the name of the chair makes reference to the shanty towns, or *favelas*, that are a feature of the outskirts of major cities such as Rio de Janeiro and São Paulo.

Below: *Lathe VIII* (2008), by the Amsterdam-based designer Sebastian Brajkovic (1975–), seeks to subvert the traditional form of the love seat. The piece – made in bronze and featuring intricate hand embroidery, and one of an edition of just eight – is now in the collection of the Victoria and Albert Museum, London.

Right: London-based Dutch designer Tord Boontje (1968–) is well known for his use of laser-cut floral and graphic forms. The Petit Jardin chair (edition of ten) transforms the chair into a garden glade and infuses it with a narrative quality. The chair is made of laser-cut steel, with a zinc and white powder coating.

Process

The chair as a basic form dates back thousands of years. Although few examples survive, sculpture, wall paintings and other sources reveal that chairs were a feature of ancient societies in Egypt, Greece, Rome and elsewhere, where they were most commonly associated with authority. As seats of power or privilege, they were often richly carved, decorated and made out of precious materials such as ebony, ivory and gold. By contrast, most of Asia, excluding China, never developed a chair-sitting culture at all, and floor-sitting remained the norm.

Chairs retained their status as power seats for many centuries, with ordinary people sitting on stools or benches or high-backed settles. It was not until the sixteenth century, with the advent of the Renaissance, that the chair began to come into common or everyday use. Ever since, the form of the chair has reflected changes in technology and materials, as much as changes in style, culture and society.

Right: This funerary stele or monument from the Kerameikos Museum in Athens, dating back to c400 BC, shows a servant handing a jewellery box to a woman seated on a *klismos* chair. The sweeping form of the sabre legs was much copied by neoclassical designers in the late eighteenth and early nineteenth centuries.

Left: Rajasthani women seated at the Bhainsrorgarh Fort Hotel. In many Eastern cultures, floor-sitting remains the norm.

23

The rise of comfort

Much early European furniture, including chairs, consisted of solid wooden panels – which were often carved or decorated in some way – enclosed within a jointed or pegged wooden framework. Some time in the seventeenth century, the 'back stool', or chair without arms, appeared. Up until that point, a chair was specifically an armchair.

The eighteenth century saw the introduction to Europe of the tropical hardwood mahogany. Before this, oak, walnut and beech had been the favoured furniture woods, and the simple chairs found in ordinary houses were often made by itinerant turners. By the seventeenth century, however, oak stocks had significantly diminished, owing to its widespread use in shipbuilding. Walnut, which superseded oak, was structurally weak and prone to woodworm. Mahogany, imported from the West Indies, proved to be an ideal wood for furniture. Dense, close-grained, worm-free and easy to carve, mahogany could be used to make much stronger chairs than before and allowed greater stylistic expression. The widespread adoption of this new material coincided with the rise of cabinetmakers, who challenged the former supremacy of joiners, and who introduced new jointing methods such as dovetailing.

Comfort was an increasing preoccupation of the age. Upholsterers, whose former role had been to create testers (canopies) and hangings for beds, began to work more closely with furniture-makers, covering and padding the seats, backs and arms of chairs and settees. Chair backs were slightly inclined to support the back; seats were wide enough to accommodate voluminous skirts and coats. The French bergère, with padded sides, and the fauteuil, with padded elbows, were typical of the new types of upholstered chair and quickly spread far beyond their native country. Similarly the English wing chair, with padded back, seat, arms and side-wings, was both enclosing and an effective shield against chilly draughts.

If chairs became much more comfortable in the eighteenth century, they were also the vehicle for variations in style, specifically in the shape and design of the back splat. In Britain, Thomas Chippendale (1718–79), one of the most famous and successful furniture-makers of the period, produced chairs whose back splats featured characteristic scrolled carving. His rival George Hepplewhite (1727–86) was associated with the shield back, and also produced oval, heart and lyre shapes. The neoclassical designs that appared towards the end of the period, such as those by Thomas Sheraton (1751–1806), were more upright, restrained and rectilinear. Pattern books, such as Chippendale's *Gentleman and Cabinet-maker's Director*, published in 1754, and Hepplewhite's *The Cabinet-maker and Upholsterer's Guide* (1788), while intended to advertise the skills of the cabinetmaker, also promoted new fashions to a growing middle-class market.

Below: *A Gentleman at Breakfast* (c1775–80), attributed to Henry Walton, oil on canvas (63.5 x 77.2 cm). While eighteenth-century design was characterized by a classically inspired elegance and restraint, comfort was also a preoccupation. The chairs pictured here have loose checked linen covers.

Chair legs underwent a similar transformation. During the early part of the eighteenth century, the typical form was the cabriole leg, which curved gently and ended in a ball-and-claw foot. While the curve of the cabriole leg was a reference to the animal legs on Greek and Roman furniture, and reflected the dominant influence of classical design, the ball and claw is thought to be Chinese in origin, representing a three-clawed dragon foot holding a pearl. Gradually, chair legs became straight and tapering, and were sometimes fluted or reeded. By the early nineteenth century, the sweeping line of the sabre leg recalled the curved legs of the Greek *klismos*, an armless chair with a shaped back rest.

The eighteenth century was characterized by a proliferation of different furniture types, and chairs were no exception. Dining chairs were produced in even-numbered sets. Side chairs, designed to be stood against a wall, were generally upholstered to match the rest of a room's furnishings. The corner chair allowed men to sit astride; the conversation chair, in which you sat back to front, had a padded top rail for lounging against. As chairs changed, so did the way interiors were arranged. Although order and symmetry remained the governing principle, and chairs were often set back against the wall when not in use, groupings gradually became more natural and furniture began to assume greater personality.

By the turn of the century it was taken for granted that chairs should be expressive, and display what the contemporary writer and art collector Thomas Hope called 'appropriate meaning'. In some ways, they also became records of changing tastes. The Trafalgar chair, with its nautical detailing, commemorated Nelson's famous victory of 1805. Spindly bamboo or beech chairs painted to resemble bamboo reflected a craze for chinoiserie. New archaeological discoveries at Pompeii and Herculaneum and a burgeoning interest in ancient Egypt were also reflected in chair detailing and form.

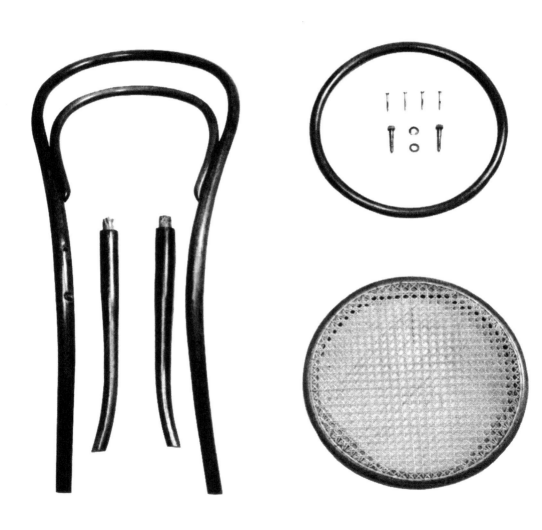

Left: A revolution in the making: Thonet's bentwood chair (No. 14, 1855) consisted of simple curved elements made of steamed wood, that could be packed flat, transported all over the world and assembled very easily using a few screws.

Below right: A page from a 1895 Thonet catalogue showing various bentwood rockers. The original Thonet company was based in Vienna with factories all around the Austro Hungarian empire, built close to timber growing areas. There are now many firms manufacturing versions of its original designs, and two successors, an Austrian and a German business. The German Thonet is based in Frankenberg where it is still run by fifth-generation family members. Thonet now produces furniture by contemporary designers, as well as classics in bentwood and tubular steel.

The birth of the modern chair

Although some mechanization was introduced early on, notably steam-powered veneer cutters and rotary cutters for producing chamfered edges, furniture-making remained largely a piecework industry throughout the nineteenth century. The unity of classicism gave way to an eclectic free-for-all, with competing Greek, gothic, Tudor, naturalistic and Louis XIV styles spelled out in elaborate ornament and detail.

Meanwhile a quiet revolution was underway. The most radical innovation of the period, and a huge technological and typological leap forward, was Thonet's bentwood chair No. 14 (1855). In 1830 the Austrian craftsman Michael Thonet (1796–1871) began experimenting with ways to produce furniture without time-consuming and costly carving and jointing. At first he used heat and water to bend thin strips of wood, which were then laminated together. Eventually he patented a process for steaming solid wood, which was bent into shape to create chair components that could simply be screwed together. A further advantage was that the chairs could be packed flat and transported around the world.

GEBRÜDER THONET

Also known as the *Konsomstuhl* ('bistro chair'), Thonet's No. 14 was produced to supply a growing international demand for café chairs. Consisting of six pieces of steamed bentwood, heated and pressed in curved cast-iron moulds, it was held together by ten screws and two nuts. Seats were often made of woven cane or palm. The chair was an immediate critical and commercial success: more than 50 million were sold between 1860 and 1930. The Thonet chair was economical, light, strong, easy to assemble and easy to repair. Still in production and widely imitated, it is arguably the most successful chair of all time, the 'chair of chairs' in the estimation of many designers and critics. 'Never was a better and more elegant design and a more precisely crafted and practical item created,' observed Le Corbusier.

The second half of the nineteenth century saw the emergence of other chair archetypes, what one might call 'designs without designers'. Into this category fall stick-back Windsor chairs, produced in both England and America, Shaker ladder-backs and rockers, and lightweight folding camp chairs and deck chairs to serve the needs of travellers and soldiers. A similar vernacular influence can be detected in various chairs produced by Morris & Co in the 1860s, such as the rush-bottomed Sussex chair, a design that fell into the category of what William Morris termed 'necessary workaday furniture'.

Right: Sussex rush-seated chairs produced by Morris & Co were copies of vernacular designs that had been seen in Sussex by the firm's business manager, Warington Taylor. Morris & Co first produced the Sussex range in 1866, with many of the chairs selling for just a few shillings. In 1865, Taylor wrote to the architect Philip Webb: 'It is hellish wickedness to spend more than 15 shillings on a chair when the poor are starving in the streets.'

THE SUSSEX RUSH-SEATED CHAIRS
MORRIS AND COMPANY
449 OXFORD STREET, LONDON, W.

"ROSSETTI ARM-CHAIR. IN BLACK, 16/6.

SUSSEX CORNER CHAIR. IN BLACK, 10/6.

SUSSEX SINGLE CHAIR. IN BLACK, 7/-.

SUSSEX ARM-CHAIR. IN BLACK, 9/9.

ROUND-SEAT CHAIR. IN BLACK, 10/6.

SUSSEX SETTEE, 4 FT. 6 IN. LONG. IN BLACK, 35/-.

ROUND SEAT PIANO CHAIR. IN BLACK, 10/6.

"Of all the specific minor improvements in common household objects due to Morris, the rush-bottomed Sussex chair perhaps takes the first place. It was not his own invention, but was copied with trifling improvements from an old chair of village manufacture picked up in Sussex. With or without modification it has been taken up by all the modern furniture manufacturers, and is in almost universal use. But the Morris pattern of the later type (there were two) still excels all others in simplicity and elegance of proportion."

"Life of William Morris" : By Prof. J. W. Mackail.

63

The machine age

The second phase of modern chair design had to wait until the early decades of the twentieth century. Early European proto-modernist groups, such as the Wiener Werkstätte and the Dutch De Stijl, had been heavily influenced by the notion of honesty of construction that was central to the Arts and Crafts movement. Gerrit Rietveld's (1888–1964) Red/Blue chair, designed in 1917–18, makes its means of assembly explicit through bisecting horizontal and vertical planes, while expressing the abstract geometric forms that appear in the paintings of fellow De Stijl member Piet Mondrian.

By the time the Bauhaus had been founded in Dessau, Germany, in 1919, mass production, and more specifically the machine, suggested a new way forward. Aeroplanes, bicycles and steamships were points of reference: form, for furniture as much as houses, followed function. For Walter Gropius, the founder of the Bauhaus, 'in order to create something that functions properly – a container, a chair, a house – its essence has to be explored…'

Below left: Marcel Breuer's tubular steel B32 chair 1928). The occupant, thought to be either Lis Beyer or Ise Gropius, is wearing a mask by the painter and sculptor Oskar Schlemmer.

Below: Mart Stam's S33 chair. Stamm was working on a prototype for a tubular steel chair as early as 1924.

Right: The Red/Blue chair (1918) by Gerrit Rietveld is an expression of planar geometry that clearly reflects the principles of the De Stijl group, and painter, Mondrian.

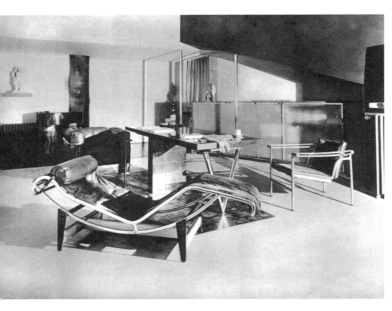

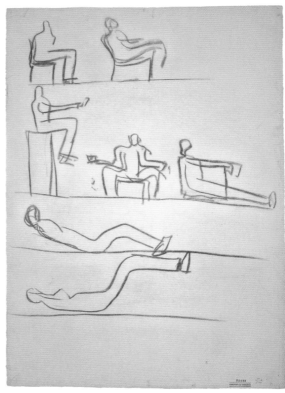

Left above: Le Corbusier and Charlotte Perriand designed the iconic Chaise Longue (B306) for the interior of Le Corbusier's modernist masterpiece Maison La Roche in Paris. Many modernist chairs were designed as part of an integrated approach to architecture and interior design.

Far left: Mies van der Rohe designed the cantilevered-steel Brno chair (MR50, 1929–30) for a bedroom in the Villa Tugendhat, in Brno (now Czech Republic).

Left: Le Corbusier sketches of seating and reclining positions, made during a lecture he gave in Buenos Aires in 1929 and published in *Précisions sur un état présent de l'architecture et de l'urbanisme*.

The idea of a tubular steel cantilever chair seems to have occurred to three designers at about the same time: Mart Stam (1899–1996), Marcel Breuer (1902–81) and Ludwig Mies van der Rohe (1886–1969), two of whom (Breuer and Mies) were at the Bauhaus. In a cantilever chair, the dual springy supports of a bent-metal framework replace the four legs and take the weight of the body front to back. Tubular steel was then a new industrial material. Breuer claimed that the idea for using it in furniture design was inspired by the lightness and strength of the tubular framework of his Adler bicycle. 'Metal furniture', he wrote,

> is part of a modern room. It is 'styleless', for it is expected not to express any particular styling beyond its purpose and the construction thereofore… This metal furniture is intended to be nothing but a necessary apparatus for contemporary life.

Of the three, Breuer's B32 chair (1928) has been the most commercially successful. Mies van der Rohe's Brno chair (MR50, 1929–30), a development of earlier ideas, is arguably the most refined. Stam's S33 chair may well have been the first: he was working on a prototype as early as 1924, fashioning the framework from lengths of gas pipes connected with elbow joints because he did not have access to the technology that would enable him to bend a continuous length of tubing.

Le Corbusier, who was so taken with the Thonet bentwood chair as a standardized functional object or 'furniture-type', in the late 1920s produced a number of iconic pieces in collaboration with Charlotte Perriand (1903–99) that were directly influenced by the mechanistic vocabulary of the Bauhaus designs. In *Précisions sur un état présent de l'architecture et de l'urbanisme* ('Reflections on the Present State of Architecture and Urbanism', 1930) he wrote:

> You sit in an active way to work… the chair must keep you awake… I sit down to talk; a chair of such and such a kind will give me a civilized posture; I sit in an active way to demonstrate a thesis, put my point of view – a high chair corresponds to my

posture… But here is a machine for resting – we have made it from bicycle tubes and covered it in a magnificent ponyskin; it is light enough to move at a touch… I thought of the cowboy in the Wild West, smoking his pipe, his feet in the air…

Le Corbusier's 'machine for resting' was the famous Chaise Longue (B306, 1928). When the chair was first published, the photograph showed a reclining Perriand in a pose of barely disguised eroticism – a far cry from a cowboy smoking a pipe. The Chaise Longue was exhibited at the 1929 Salon d'automne in Paris, at the same time as his 'comfort-machine', Le Grand Confort (LC2, 1928), where the tubular steel framework is expressed on the outside rather than being concealed by upholstery. There were hopes of putting these, and other designs, into mass production, and Le Corbusier offered them to Peugeot, reckoning that the extensive use of tubular steel in the framework would make chairs a natural choice for a mass-producer of bicycles. Peugeot turned them down and they were taken up instead by Thonet, which however never manufactured more than a limited number of pieces.

Le Corbusier's designs, like many other early modernist chairs, have had a chequered history of production. Ironically, designs inspired by and intended for mass manufacture had to wait until much later before they reached a wider market, and even then many have remained expensive.

Right: This 1970s Knoll magazine advertisement for the Barcelona chair (1929), designed by Mies van der Rohe and Lilly Reich (1885–1947), plays on its status as an icon of 1920s modernist design.

Below: The Bibendum chair (1929) by the Irish designer Eileen Gray (1878–1976) was one of a number of modernist pieces she designed for her own house, E-1027, at Roquebrune-Cap-Martin in the south of France, which she built between 1926 and 1929 in collaboration with Jean Badovici.

In 1929, Mies Van Der Rohe designed the Barcelona Chair.
See it at The Museum of Modern Art in New York,
and buy it through Knoll Showrooms in 28 countries.

Knoll Associates, Inc., Furniture and Textiles, 320 Park Avenue, New York 10022.
The 1929 Fortuny Gown, courtesy of The Brooklyn Museum

Left: Alvar Aalto's classic three-legged stool (Model No. 60, 1932–3) features his innovative L-leg. The leg could be screwed directly to the underside of a seat, doing away with joinery or supporting framework.

Below: Constructing the L-leg, a bentwood leg made of Finnish birch that was an essential component of many of Aalto's designs. Solid timber was sawn in the direction of the fibres to form a fan-shape. Thin pieces of veneer were then glued into the grooves so the wood could be bent through 90 degrees with the aid of heat and steam.

Bentwood revisited

When modernist ideals spread north to Scandinavia, the industrial aesthetic developed into a more approachable style. One reason for this was the enduring and deep-rooted influence of natural forms on Scandinavian design. Another was the fact that there was very little heavy industry in these countries at the time, which ruled out the manufacture of metal furniture. Wood, however, was an abundant local resource.

A leading figure in modern furniture design between the world wars was the Finnish architect and designer Alvar Aalto. From 1929, with his wife Aino (1894–1949) and Otto Korhonen, a technical director of a furniture factory, Aalto embarked upon experiments and researches into moulding and bending wood. He was concerned to marry the purity and functionalism of modernism with the warmth of wood. For ease and economy of manufacture as much as for visual clarity, he was also interested in producing furniture with the fewest possible number of elements. A key development in this process was the 'L-leg' – 'the little sister of the architectonic column', as Aalto called it. This strong bentwood element could be attached directly to the underside of a seat, doing away with a supporting framework. It most famous application is in the three-legged stool (Model No. 60, 1932–3).

Another seminal design was the Paimio lounge chair (1930–1), designed as part of Aalto's Paimio Sanitorium. The single scrolling piece of laminated ply that forms the back and seat is hung from a solid-birch bentwood frame. Easy to massproduce, the chair won Aalto international recognition when it was exhibited at London's Fortnum & Mason department store in London in 1933. Critical success and good sales led the Aaltos to set up their own manufacturing company, Artek, in 1935, with the stated aim of bringing 'a human perspective to modernism'.

Mid-century modern

Right: Hans Wegner's Y or Wishbone chair (1950) is a classic of Danish design, showing the characteristic Scandinavian modern marriage of organic form and clean simple lines.

By the end of the World War II, modernism had won the argument. In America, European architects and designers including Mies van der Rohe, Walter Gropius and Eliel Saarinen (1873–1950), who had emigrated to the USA before the war, exerted their influence on a new generation. Saarinen, the first director of the Cranbrook Academy of Art in Michigan, was instigative in promoting a progressive yet human-centred approach to design.

When the work of new designers from Sweden, Denmark and Finland crossed the Atlantic in the immediate postwar years, the ground had already been prepared. At the same time, conditions were right for the emergence of home-grown talent, such as Eliel's son Eero (1910–61), Harry Bertoia (1915–78), Ray (1912–88) and Charles (1907–78) Eames, and Florence Knoll (1917–), all alumni of the Cranbrook Academy.

'Danish modern', as the new Scandinavian style was at first called, had an immediate appeal that soon broadened out across all market levels. The Danish furniture designers Hans Wegner (1914–2007) and Finn Juhl (1912–89) were the first to gain widespread attention and acclaim. The defining material of the new style was teak. After the Second World War there was a surplus of this tropical hardwood, owing to the extensive logging for military purposes in mainland Southeast Asia, and Denmark was one of its chief importers. As a hardwood, teak requires little finishing; it is also very strong and stable.

Wegner and Juhl, who had come out of Denmark's craft-based furniture-making tradition, devised new jointing techniques for teak that allowed them to express fluid, flowing curves in their designs. They were also directly influenced by the research carried out between the wars by the Danish architect and furniture designer Kaare Klint (1888–1954), who had studied the human form closely in order to come up with the proportions and dimensions on which he believed furniture design should be based.

Left: Wegner's Round chair (1949), highly acclaimed as soon as it was produced, illustrates the designer's tireless pursuit of the ideal chair form, as well as his mastery of jointing techniques to achieve flowing curves. Originally produced in teak, it is now made in a range of other hardwoods.

Below right: The American broadcaster CBS bought 12 Round chairs for the set of the first televised presidential candidate debates between Senator John F. Kennedy and Vice-President Richard Nixon (26 September 1960).

The prolific Wegner was responsible for more than five hundred chair designs, and was dedicated to an ideal of perfection: 'The good chair is a task one is never completely done with.' The Round chair (PP501/503, 1949) arguably came closest to his aim. Described as the 'world's most beautiful chair' when it featured in the American magazine *Interiors* in 1950, ten years later it was chosen as seating for the televised debates between presidential candidates John F. Kennedy and Richard Nixon.

Another hugely influential Danish designer was Arne Jacobsen, responsible for the Ant chair (1951–2), the Series 7, Model 3107 chair (1955), and the iconic Egg chair (1958), among many others. The Ant chair and Model 3107 chair were made out of moulded plywood; while the technique was far from new, Jacobsen's notorious perfectionism and his desire to achieve the most minimal use of material placed considerable demands on the production process. For the Ant chair, Jacobsen modelled the design first in clay and went through some ten prototypes: 'I myself stood and modelled it to achieve the right curves, which are decisive for the

43

Arne Jacobsen's Model 3107 chair (1955) has been one of the most commercially successful chairs of all time. The design began as a variant on the previous Ant series and then evolved into a series of its own. Today the chair is produced in a huge range of colours and finishes, including leather and fabric upholstered versions. The leather version is shown here. The chair has a quirky individuality that enables it to be used both on its own and in serried ranks.

Left and below: The Model 3107 chair in production at the Danish manufacturer Fritz Hansen. The seat and back are made of a single moulded shell, consisting of nine layers of birch veneer with two layers of cotton textile sandwiched in between. The base is steel. Jacobsen designed a range of eight bright colours for the chair in 1968, a colour range that was extended by Verner Panton in 1972.

Below: Components of the Lounge chair (670) and Ottoman (671) designed by Charles and Ray Eames in 1956. The three moulded plywood shells are veneered in rosewood; the cushions are filled with foam and down and upholstered in leather.

Following pages: Sales poster (c.1952) produced by the Eames Office for the Herman Miller Furniture Co. to advertise their plywood, fibreglass and wire chair and table configurations.

seating position. We cannot see the cut, but we feel it. It is right if we rest in it. Then we can make the chair's appearance correspond to our view of what looks good.' The Model 3107 chair, which began as a variant of the Ant, and which like the Ant is still in production, has sold five million units to date. The Egg chair, designed for Jacobsen's SAS Royal Hotel, Copenhagen, is an essay in curves, a modern version of the classic wing chair. Like many of the best Scandinavian designs of the period, it marries purity of form with an organic warmth and approachability. It seems to ask you to sit in it.

The same organic humanism can be seen in the work of Eero Saarinen and Charles and Ray Eames. Charles Eames had begun experimenting with moulded ply in the late 1930s. In 1940 he and Saarinen, a close friend, co-designed a moulded plywood chair that won first prize at the Museum of Modern Art's 'Organic Designs in Home Furnishings' competition. During the Second World War Charles Eames designed leg splints and stretchers made of moulded plywood for the US Navy, while his wife Ray made plywood sculptures, and these projects directly informed

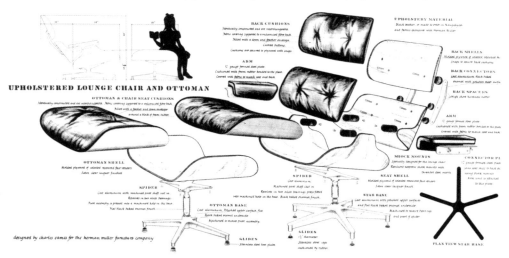

WOOD   PLASTIC   WIRE   CHAIRS

herman
miller
furniture
company
CHAIRS
zeeland
michigan

designed
by
charles
eames

& TABLES   WOOD   PLASTIC   WIRE

COMBINING BEAUTY AND UTILITY...THE CHARLES EAMES MOLDED PLYWOOD CHAIR

AIRPLANE MANUFACTURING TECHNIQUES LED TO THE MOLDED PLASTIC ARMCHAIR

NEWEST CONTRIBUTION TO LOW-COST SEATING COMFORT: THE UPHOLSTERED WIRE CHAIR

48

INCORPORATING REVOLUTIONARY PRINCIPLES IN BOTH DESIGN AND CONSTRUCTION, THESE CHAIRS AND TABLES DESIGNED BY CHARLES EAMES HAVE WON WORLD-WIDE ACCLAIM AS FOREMOST EXPRESSIONS OF GOOD MODERN DESIGN. THEIR EXCEPTIONAL COMFORT, PRACTICALITY AND CRISP SILHOUETTES, COUPLED WITH THEIR EXTREMELY MODEST PRICES, HAVE GAINED THEM A CONSTANTLY EXPANDING ACCEPTANCE FROM COAST TO COAST.

THESE CHAIRS AND TABLES CAN BE PURCHASED THROUGH FURNITURE DEALERS EVERYWHERE. ON VIEW AT OUR SHOWROOMS IN NEW YORK, CHICAGO, GRAND RAPIDS, KANSAS CITY AND LOS ANGELES.

herman miller furniture company

TABLES   PLYWOOD AND PLASTIC TABLES FOR MANY USES ARE AN IMPORTANT PART OF THE EAMES GROUP. DINING, CARD, COFFEE AND INCIDENTAL TABLES ARE INCLUDED, SEVERAL WITH FOLDING OR DETACHABLE LEGS.

DCM	DCW	LCM	LCW

dining chair
rod base
seat ht. — 17¾"

dining chair
wood base
seat ht. — 17½"

lounge chair
rod base
seat ht. — 15½"

lounge chair
wood base
seat ht. — 15½"

WOOD: MOLDED PLYWOOD SEATS AND BACKS, ATTACHED BY RUBBER SHOCK MOUNTS TO FRAMES OF HEAVILY PLATED METAL OR WOOD, YIELD A RESILIENCE AND COMFORT NORMALLY FOUND ONLY IN UPHOLSTERED CHAIRS. AVAILABLE IN WALNUT, BIRCH, CALICO ASH, RED OR BLACK, IN LOUNGE AND DINING HEIGHTS.

FINISHES

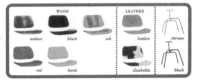

WOOD — *walnut, black, ash, red, birch*
LEATHER — *leather, skunkskin*
chrome, black

DAR	PAW	DAR	DAX	SAX	RAR	LAX	LAR

or desk chair
wire base
at ht. — 17⅞"

swivel chair
wood base
seat ht. — 17⅞"

dining or desk chair
wood base
seat ht. — 17⅞"

dining or desk chair
rod base
seat ht. — 17⅞"

standard height chair
rod base
seat ht. — 16¾"

rocking chair
rocker base
seat ht. — 16"

lounge chair
rod base
seat ht. — 14⅞"

low lounge chair
wire base
seat ht. — 12¼"

PLASTIC: A PLASTIC REINFORCED WITH FIBERGLAS IS SKILFULLY MOLDED TO FORM AN EXCEPTIONALLY COMFORTABLE AND VIRTUALLY INDESTRUCTIBLE ARMCHAIR. THE PLASTIC SHELL COMES IN EIGHT ATTRACTIVE COLORS; CHOICE OF SIX DIFFERENT BASES, OF BOTH WOOD AND METAL, INCLUDING A ROCKER AND SWIVEL DESK CHAIR.

FINISHES

INTEGRAL COLORS — *red, elephant hide grey, lemon yellow, parchment, greige, sea foam green*
APPLIED COLORS — *dark blue, neutral grey*
zinc, black, birch, walnut

DKR	PKW	DKW	RKR	LKX	LKR

or desk chair
wire base
at ht. — 18½"

swivel chair
wood base
seat ht. — 17⅞"

dining or desk chair
wood base
seat ht. — 17⅞"

rocking chair
rocker base
seat ht. — 17"

lounge chair
rod base
seat ht. — 16"

low lounge chair
wire base
seat ht. — 13"

WIRE: A MOLDED WIRE SHELL, UPHOLSTERED WITH A ONE OR TWO PIECE CUSHION, EASILY REMOVABLE, OFFERS EXCEPTIONAL SEATING COMFORT AT LOW COST. CUSHIONS CAN BE HAD IN A GOOD-LOOKING TEXTURED FABRIC OR GENUINE LEATHER. THERE ARE SIX BASES, EMPLOYING BOTH METAL AND WOOD, IN STYLES SUITABLE FOR DINING, READING AND LOUNGING.

FINISHES

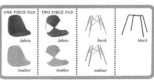

ONE PIECE PAD — *fabric, leather*
TWO PIECE PAD — *fabric, leather*
birch, walnut, black

CUSHION IS EASILY REMOVED FROM WIRE SHELL. CUSHIONS ARE INTERCHANGEABLE.

the design of a number of moulded plywood chairs they produced after the war. Both the DCM and the LCW (1946) won instant critical acclaim and were the beginning of a fruitful collaboration with the progressive US furniture company Herman Miller.

Like the famous Eames House (properly known as Case Study House #8, 1949), which made radical use of prefabricated elements, there is something of a kit-of-parts quality to these designs. The original intention was to make a chair that consisted of a single shell of moulded plywood, but the material was unable to withstand the stresses where the seat met the back. Instead, bent and welded metal mesh proved a better way of achieving a single-shell design that could be massproduced. The Eameses' DKR Wire Mesh chair (1951) is contoured to support the body. To keep costs low, the rim of the chair is made of lighter-gauge wire doubled up. Harry Bertoia's Diamond chair (1952–3) was a similar essay in lightness and transparency.

During the 1950s and 1960s, the work of Italian designers equalled the best that emerged from Scandinavia, both in quality of manufacture and commitment to modernity. In Italy, a progressive approach to design had been the defining element of postwar reconstruction, led by foward-thinking companies such as Cassina and Artemide. The Superleggera chair (1957) by Giò Ponti (1891–1979) was derived from the *chiavari* chair, a vernacular fisherman's chair. The Modello 15 chair (1964) by Vico Magistretti (1920–2006), with its red painted frame and rush seating, had similar vernacular antecedents.

Left and below: The Swiss designer Hans Coray (1907–91) is best known for his Landi chair (1938), a design that came about as the result of a commission for the Swiss National Exhibition of 1939, which required to him to create an aluminium chair that could be used both indoors and out. The graphic holes increase the lightness of the design – the chair weighs just 3kg.

Right: Giò Ponti's Superleggera chair (1957) was influenced by the *chiavari*, or fishermen's chairs seen on Italian beaches. It is so strong and light it can be lifted with one finger.

conversation, rest & play

Gondola,Comfortable,Duchesse,Psyche,Kangaroo; are some names of the past for a type of seating that fills a difficult-to-define need of the time.

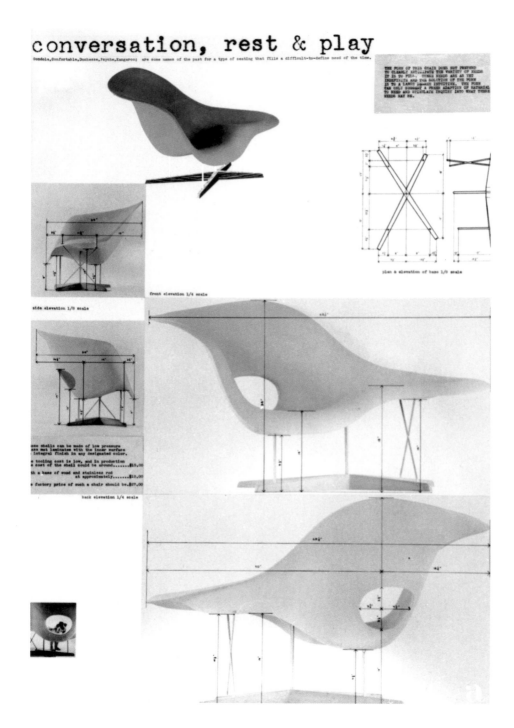

plan & elevation of base 1/8 scale

front elevation 1/4 scale

side elevation 1/8 scale

back elevation 1/4 scale

ese shells can be made of low pressure.
ass mat laminates with the inner surface
  integral finish in any designated color.

e tooling cost is low, and in production
a cost of the shell could be around......$15.00

th a base of wood and stainless rod
              at approximately.......$12.00

e factory price of such a chair should be.$27.00

54

Left: La Chaise by Charles
and Ray Eames (1948) was
the first chair in which the
plastic shell was exposed.
The shell was made of
fibreglass-reinforced plastic.

Plastic

Any new material seems to inspire designers to make a chair out
of it. In the immediate postwar period, plastic was viewed as a
progressive futuristic material, and its mouldable quality opened
up exciting new possibilities. The Eameses, who were constantly
experimenting with technology, produced one of the first plastic
chairs in which the surface of the shell is exposed. This was La
Chaise ('The Chair'), created for the International Competition for
Low-cost Furniture Design held at New York's Museum of Modern
Art in 1948. With a sculpted body made of fibreglass-reinforced
plastic, the design came out of a collaboration with Zenith Plastics,
which had used fibreglass to strength the plastic on airplane radar
domes during the war. Like all of the Eameses' work, La Chaise
has tremendous personality. According to Tibor Kalman, designer
and editor, it 'exudes as much feeling of life and wholeness as a
living, breathing thing. It is alive. It can be lived with, seen every
day, change and evolve, and slowly reveal its beauty. Like a lover.
And it's a chair.'

While plastic opened up new directions, designers soon found
that their visions outstripped what was technically possible. Eero
Saarinen's Tulip chair (1955–6) is made of a moulded fibreglass
shell mounted on a cast aluminium base. Limitations of plastics
technology at the time prevented him from achieving what he had
intended, which was a single one-legged moulded form. One
design that was notoriously beset by production difficulties was
Verner Panton's (1926–98) plastic cantilever chair, its sleek glossy
curves reminiscent of car bodies. Although the original concept
dated back to 1960, the Panton chair was not put into production
until 1967, after much trial and error, and was withdrawn 12 years
later because the plastics then available were not strong enough
for the daring and demanding form. In 1990 Vitra reissued the
chair in both polypropylene and polyurethane hard foam.

One of the most commercially successful plastic chairs was
designed by Robin Day in 1962–3. The first chair to make use

55

of injection-moulded polypropylene, invented ten years earlier, and manufactured by the London furniture company Hille, the Polyprop chair consisted of a lightweight plastic shell, with a deep, curved lip to give rigidity, supported on a base of bent tubular steel. Stackable, cheap and produced in a range of colours, it has sold in millions in 23 countries around the world. The chair's rather utilitarian image as the ubiquitous seating for school halls and doctors' waiting rooms was given a makeover in the late 1990s when the armchair version of the design was reissued by Tom Dixon in pale translucent polypropylene (1959–) at the UK high-street furnishings chain Habitat. Much sleeker was the Selene chair (1968) by Vico Magistretti, made of glossy glass-reinforced plastic

SINGLE PEDESTAL FURNITURE DESIGNED BY EERO SAARINEN

Left below: Eero Saarinen's Tulip chair (1955–6) features a moulded fibreglass shell on a cast aluminium base. The original intention was to produce a single one-legged form, but the limitations of the plastics technology then available prevented this.

Right: The Blow chair (1967) by Jonathan de Pas, Donato D'Urbino, Paolo Lomazzi and Carla Scolari is the original version of the much-imitated inflatable plastic chair. Made of welded PVC, it reflects the designers' intention of debunking the iconic status of the chair, as well as the influence of Pop art.

Below: Lord Yo (1994) by Philippe Starck is one of a number of Starck designs from this period that used polypropylene to create chairs of lightness, poise and refinement.

Left: Robin Day's Polypropylene, or Polyprop, chair (1963), a stackable utilitarian design, was the first to make use of injection-moulded polypropylene, a material invented in 1953.

Right: The Selene chair (1968) by Vico Magistretti was the first Italian injection-moulded design. It is made of glass-reinforced plastic and features a sleek S-shaped leg section.

and featuring an innovative S-shaped leg section. Chic, sculptural and affordable, this injection-moulded stacking chair was the first Italian design of its kind.

By the 1990s, however, plastic had become associated with everything that was cheap, nasty and disposable. That all changed when the French designer Philippe Starck (1949–) produced his first plastic chairs. Designs such as Lord Yo (1994) and Dr No (1996) played with traditional chair forms. The minimal use of polypropylene gave them lightness and refinement, while their finely judged flares and curves dispelled any hint of shoddiness or second-best. Nothing about the quantity in which such designs could be produced, or in their relatively low cost, diminished their quality. Plastic had acquired nobility and finesse.

The impact of Starck's designs instigated a new interest in plastic among furniture designers, as well as a race to produce the first monoblock plastic chair. It also altered the outlook of manufacturers, who were increasingly prepared to see the economic point of investing in a mould. Starck's early plastic chairs made use of standard plastic technology. Jasper Morrison's Air-chair (1999) was ground-breaking in its use of gas-injection moulding. Injecting gas into a mould pushes the plastic material to the edges and creates a hollow, which means that it is possible to change the sections so that chair legs can be a certain thickness, seats thinner and backrests thinner still. These changes in section produce designs that feel like they have more volume. The Air-chair – light, durable and innovative – is a classic example of how an advance in technology can result in a new design language.

Framed and jointed, carved and padded, bent and moulded, fashioned out of wood, tubular steel, metal mesh or plastic, throughout history the form of chair has always revealed an intimate connection with material and process.

Right: Verner Panton's cantilever chair (1960), a plastic stacking chair with an organic form suggestive of a car body, proved notoriously difficult to produce. First issued seven years after it was designed, the chair was withdrawn from production 12 years later and was reissued only in 1990.

60

The Air chair (1999) by Jasper Morrison was ground-breaking in its use of gas-injection moulding, and ushered in a new design language. Gas injection permits changes in section because the plastic material is pushed to the edges of the mould, creating a hollow.

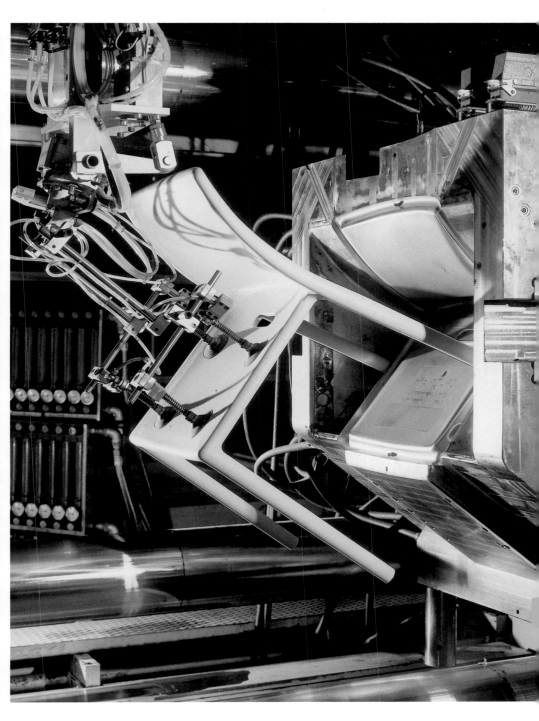

The 'Corrupted Classics' series by the London-based conceptual artist John Angelo Benson (1971–) offers a subversive look at the icons of chair design.

Below: Mies Lobby Trap. Year: 2003. Material: Stainless steel spikes, Barcelona chair produced by Knoll. Dimensions: 77 (h) x 75 (w) x 76cm (d).

Right above: Red/Blue But Clear Chair. Year: 2003. Material: Perspex. Dimensions: 88 (h) x 65.5 (w) x 83cm (d).

Right below: Naked Confort Year: 2003. Material: Hay, Petit Confort (LC2) frame produced by Cassina. Dimensions: 67 (h) x 76 (w) x 70cm (d).

Case study:
Myto

Designer:
Konstantin Grcic

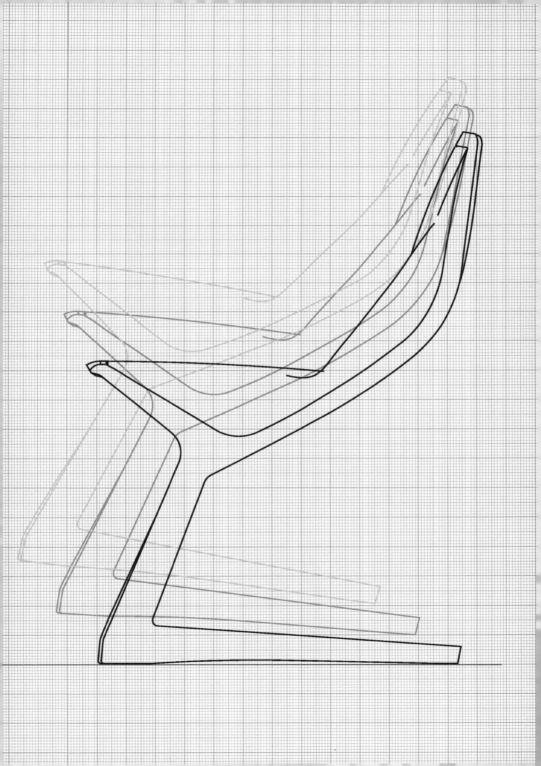

Interview with Konstantin Grcic

Born in Munich in 1965, Konstantin Grcic studied carpentry and cabinetmaking at Parnham College in Dorset (1985–7) before taking a master's degree in industrial design at the Royal College of Art in London (1988–90). After graduating he spent a year in Jasper Morrison's studio before returning to Munich to found his own practice, Konstantin Grcic Industrial Design (KGID), in 1991.

KGID has established a leading reputation in various fields of design, ranging from furniture and industrial products to exhibition design and architecture-related work, collaborating with well-known producers such as Authentics, Capellini, Iittala, Flos, Krups, Muji and Magis. A number of Grcic's products have won international design awards – in 2001 his Mayday lamp won the influential Compasso d'Oro – and his designs form part of the permanent collections of many of the world's leading museums.

Grcic defines function in human terms, and his designs are always grounded in the way people will respond to and use the finished product. Earlier designs featured a strictly rationalist approach; more recently he has used computer design software to create more fluid forms. A passion for technology and materials, as well as simplicity, characterizes all his work.

*What attracts you to chairs? You've done quite a few,
haven't you?*

Yes, we do a lot of furniture design and within furniture design
chairs are the most challenging product. They're also the most
enjoyable, somehow. A chair always has a character. It has four
legs, it has a face, it has a personality.

*You can't help but ascribe human characteristics to it
in some sense.*

Exactly, and that makes designing a chair so difficult and at the
same time so enjoyable. People sometimes ask, 'Why another
chair?' I think it's possibly because chairs are like human beings,
every one is different – sometimes only in the details, sometimes
in terms of major jumps you can make in typology or function.
Technology also plays a role.

Chairs seem to summarize aspects of society, don't they?

Absolutely. Chairs change with society. You can tell design history
by chairs but also you can tell a lot about different cultures – if they
have chairs at all. Who is actually sitting on them, and for how long,
and in what environment? How much formality is there in sitting?
Right now I'm sitting on the front edge and corner of the chair
talking to you, and I hope it's not impolite, me sitting like that, but
probably a hundred years ago it would have been interpreted in a
different way.

That's why designing chairs always has that attraction. It's not just
the object you work on: you have to look at the wider context and
that becomes part of the project and gives you ideas. But as a
designer you're not totally free to choose what you look into. If we
design a chair for an area in a building, is it indoors or outdoors?
If it's indoors, then where would you see that chair? There are a
million questions and they're quite obvious. There are chairs that
only need to be good enough for people to sit on for five minutes.

Or is it a chair where you're going to be sitting listening to a lecture or a concert? Is it a dining chair, at home or in a restaurant? All of these factors are fascinating and part of the design process.

How do you work with clients? Do manufacturers tend to come to you and say 'I'd like you to do a chair for us', or do you think of a direction and approach a manufacturer, or is it a bit of both?

Usually the manufacturer comes to us. We don't design just speculatively. Now I have a list of manufacturers that I work with constantly; therefore even if I have an idea, I'll immediately think of someone who could do this project with me. The process is always a dialogue. It's like a love affair. Few designers are their own producers. It's very rare. The more common model is a designer and a client, or producer. Nowadays, a lot of the companies we work with don't come to us with a concrete briefing. Projects develop out of a conversation. 'Think about the next thing we'd both like to do together.' So you need a good partner. If you look at the companies who have produced the good or important or interesting chairs in recent history, it's always those that have a kind of substance; they have the technical back-up. Designing a chair is an ambitious project and it's time-consuming.

And it requires new thought on the part of the producer?

Absolutely, and it's an intense journey that you take together. Usually what starts the project off is a certain idea of the kind of chair we want to do together. Producers have their own territories of technologies but only a few have production facilities in house. [The Italian furniture manufacturer] Plank, for example, are like editors: they're driving this development process but the actual factory is not in-house, it's a subcontractor. That creates almost a triangular relationship. They could do a wooden chair, or a metal chair, or an upholstered chair, and that's true of most companies. Only a few specialize in plastic chairs or wooden chairs. Anyway, you make that decision about materials and technology very early on in the project. Sometimes it can really be the fundamental condition; sometimes it gives direction and then changes later.

The Myto chair was very much driven by a type of plastic.

Yes, the Myto chair is not totally representative of how most of these projects operate, because the initiator of that design was the [German] chemical company BASF. They came to me and asked me to design something using their material Ultradur, and when I suggested a chair I then recruited Plank to become part of the project.

A plastic material means a certain formula, but then that formula can be manipulated to create a variety of materials with different qualities, all based on the same mother material. Ultradur wasn't new. They had been using it very successfully in the motor industry for years.

What sort of parts were they making?

All sorts of parts, from roof railings and engine parts to reflectors for headlights and so on. That shows you that from one mother formula you can really push the material in quite different ways. The car industry is the most important industry for a chemical company like BASF, but the present economic crisis shows that there's a danger of becoming too dependent on a vulnerable sector. BASF had an instinct that they wanted to promote their material in other industries – furniture, products, anything outside the motor industry represented a very attractive potential market. But they knew they'd have to communicate a lot more about who they are and what their material is, and really promote their material so that people recognized its possibilities.

So that's why they thought, OK, we need to speak to a designer. A designer will design a product and the product will advertise the plastic. The whole thing was a marketing idea – they could have spent the money on advertising. I thought it was very intelligent, very smart. They said, 'Give the designer the material to work with and we don't want a showpiece, a prototype; we want this designer to design a real commercial product because that will give credibility to our material and spread the news.'

Did they have a chair in mind when they asked you?

I don't know what they had in mind, but probably more of a product. But as soon as they told me about the structural characteristics of the material it just seemed so logical and tempting to do a chair. We could have done a bottle opener – it's quite tough, a bottle opener from plastic, but nobody would talk about a bottle opener.

A chair can stand on its own.

Exactly. When I started designing the chair, I was feeling a little uneasy. So many great plastic chairs had been designed in the 1990s – why do another one? I was really looking for motivation, not just a formal or aesthetic one, but one that was driven by this idea of performance that I had from the material. Once I came up with the idea of doing a cantilever chair, I knew immediately that this would be the project. What I didn't know until after we made our first presentation was that BASF had initiated the Panton chair project in the 1960s, which was the last plastic cantilever chair, but failed to realize it, and in the end it was their competitor who was stronger in foams who was able to achieve it.

When we made the presentation of the chair, BASF said yes, they were confident they could do it. Only now are they prepared to admit that they were quite scared at the time whether the material would be able to perform. It took them a while to make it perform. You can push the formula by adding certain ingredients – it's like cooking – and in the end they created a new material specifically for the chair, but which was still based on the mother material. That was not what they had intended to do in the beginning, but in a way it proves their point exactly. First of all, their material is so flexible that they can push to meet the exact requirements of the client.

And secondly, BASF was a partner in the whole process, and this is something that they wanted to get across – BASF is not simply the supplier of the material, but you can collaborate with them, designing your material.

I don't want to sound like I've been brainwashed into marketing their material, but it really came true, it became this ideal scenario for the product. It challenged them enormously but in the end they made it happen, and we have a chair that people recognize as something that was not really possible before. Vitra, for example, who produced the Panton chair and who are absolute experts in designing the most beautiful and advanced chairs and who had recently brought out a new version of the Panton chair with new technology, claimed it was impossible to design another kind of cantilever chair. Yet we were able to do it in this intense and fruitful collaboration between Plank, which is quite a small company, BASF and ourselves.

How did the collaboration work between BASF and Plank?

The Italians have a technique of moulding that involves applying so much pressure to the material and pushing so much into the tool that when you open the mould, the piece almost expands and then contracts to the right size. This is to avoid gas injection, which involves much higher costs. We did the same with Myto. The interesting thing was that the German plastic experts said it was impossible and it wasn't the right way to do it. We were confronting them with this Italian model of thought, which wasn't strictly speaking academic, and there was quite a debate. What convinced BASF in the end was that the cost of a gas injection tool would make the product so expensive no one would buy it.

Once you had the idea of the cantilever chair, what was the next stage? You work very much with models, don't you?

We knew something about this material, but only in an abstract sense, and although I've had experience designing with plastic, it's not like mocking up a wooden chair, where you can reproduce or simulate exactly what a production piece would be. You cannot do that with plastic, you have to find another means.

A material that is analogous?

I think certainly in this early stage you try to work in different ways and at different levels. Of course the computer gives us control over geometry and records everything we do. On the other hand, we wanted to work with a material that was mouldable, because plastic allows you to create very flowing surfaces, softer geometries. A wooden chair would be one plank joined to another. So we found this kind of metal mesh that helped us free-form and mould, and suddenly we had found a way of mocking up the idea. These are real moments of creation. You start with nothing, you build something and that process has a certain speed. It's physical activity, action really, and that has to happen fast. Whatever model-making method and material you choose, you make sure it's something that's very controllable, very easy to produce and therefore fast.

Because you're trying to catch an idea?

Yes, it's like the hand sketch. You make a lot of these models very fast. You make one and then you destroy it. Then you make the next one. You can't afford to make too beautiful a model, you can't afford to make one that takes too long or costs a lot of money. That's why we work in this quite primitive way, also using paper and cardboard a lot. It's very liberating, because what matters is that process of thinking.

Thinking with your hands…

Absolutely. And you don't want to be distracted or disturbed by any other thing. These models we are making purely for ourselves. Nobody else needs to read them or understand what they mean; they're not a presentation tool. So it's like a hand sketch – you can read your own handwriting and nobody else has to. The computer follows this whole process in parallel. Whatever we change directly on the model, we input into the computer to translate the geometry into 3D data. After four weeks, we had the general design direction.

That's working at a furious pace.

The project was under a certain pressure of time, which was good. I don't think we were going so fast that we would run the risk of making compromises to achieve these deadlines. This kind of project is so exciting – you're so passionate about it, you become almost impatient to make progress and that speeds things up. The physical approach of making mock-ups makes things so much clearer. If the design process is a process of decision-making, it's much easier to make decisions in that kind of scenario. You make something and you look at it and you can make a judgment on it – OK, we need to cut something off here, or we need to add something there – and that's how you propel yourself forward.

If you just sit in front of a computer or a piece of paper, it's a lot more difficult. This is more reassuring. The models are free-standing, full-scale. A chair is not an isolated product. Even at an early stage you want to have the sensation of seeing it from different angles, from the far end of the studio. All these observations are really important. Seeing it in relation to a table or another chair or to a human tells me a lot. Does it feel big? Does it feel too small?

You also made polystyrene models.

We made polystyrene models because we wanted to sit on the chair, not only to test posture and ergonomics, but also to see what it looks like with somebody sitting in it. In this process we have to make sure we never lose contact with all these simple things. The more we can simulate them or test them and work as close as possible to the real thing, the better control we have over the process and the result. It's what I enjoy about design – it relates so much to the everyday … it's all common sense. Everyone knows a lot about chairs because ever since childhood they've sat on them. I'm able to design chairs not because I know so much more, but maybe because I have spent more time thinking about them and I know what to observe. The information is nothing arcane. Designing this kind of everyday product is so beautiful because it's so real. And in the end a successful product works because people can read it and understand it why it works.

> *You spent a lot of time trying to work out the perforations as well, the patterned back?*

Oh, yes [laughs]. I had an idea about using this plastic material, which was a little bit naïve. But as a designer, my advantage over the plastics expert is that I don't know everything so I can make assumptions. BASF told me that they could push the mother material into a material that is quite flexible and delicate on the one hand, to something at the other extreme where it becomes almost like steel. So I thought we'd do a chair where we'd have both – we'd have the strength *and* the flexibility. My idea was to have a kind of outline frame as the main structural support, the strong element, with a net structure sitting in the frame in much lighter, smaller sections to provide flexibility and transparency and reduce weight. But it's all one process of moulding – it's not a case of making a frame and putting a net inside. Achieving this wasn't easy and it was one of the challenges that BASF faced.

When BASF inject the material into the mould, they can simulate on the computer exactly how it expands or flows. In technical terms, it's called the 'mould-flow'. One of the properties of this Ultradur material is that it flows very fast or easily. If you imagine the difference between honey and water, their material, they claim, is closer to water.

The mould is a kind of cavity inside a massive steel block, so the material would have to flow through all these little channels to find its way, and we could only do this using a material with a high fluidity. We thought we could design the net in any way we wanted and then they would make the tool from the drawing. At first we thought we might do something asymmetric, but we then learned from BASF that this was totally naïve and impossible.

The flow is something like aerodynamics. For every hole in this mesh there's a metal pin in the mould and the material has to find its way round it, rejoin again and then there's the next metal pin and the next. So unless we design the hole in such a way that it is aerodynamic, the material would hit the pin and create a turmoil in the flow. The people at BASF showed us the simulation and it was so revealing. We'd done things in plastic before and I'd never thought of that. Then it all became so logical and that's why the holes are oblong-shaped.

How does the mould operate?

The tool is a huge steel block that comes in two parts. The steel is extremely tempered and very hard and it is engineered into the positive and negative forms of the chair. Inside the steel are very complex heating and cooling chambers. Before injecting the material, they have to heat the steel to bring it to a certain temperature that will keep the plastic flowing, because every time the material makes contact with the steel it cools off a little.

The plastic is injected into the mould at three points at the front of the chair, and that is the result of lengthy and thorough simulation. The material will first find the way of least resistance, so it will go into the biggest sections of the mould first and then travel up the side of the chair where the sections are still quite big. As you keep pushing material into the mould, in the end it will have to travel into the net and begin to close in from the sides. The central injection point is important because it ensures there is material in the middle in the later phase of the injection.

Of course, there will be one area where the material finally closes. In some of the early attempts the material failed to close, and it was always in the same place in the seat. In the development process we had to make changes to shift this area of closure to the backrest, the part of the chair that is less structurally important and where it would be least likely to break. Basically now we have a taper in the seat, so we have a thicker section of the mesh towards the front, giving the material an easier entry here. It's very nerdy stuff but it was fascinating for us to learn. It's nice when the design process has certain constraints. They help you make decisions.

What other constraints did you have?

Cost is a factor, of course. The main issues that affect cost are the size and complexity of the mould. We were able to make this chair in a two-part mould, which is the simplest form of mould possible. A glass, which is a conical shape, could be made in a two-part mould. Most chairs have such complex shapes the mould would have to open in more parts than just two. A normal mould would be three parts, with small sliders.

We didn't really think about this at the beginning. But we were lucky that the engineer who was making the mould saw our design at an early stage when it was easy to change. Because he has an eye for how to translate a design into a mould, he suggested that if we changed something he could reduce the mould to two parts, so immediately we changed it. This makes the mould simpler and therefore less expensive – these moulds can cost 100,000 euros at least – and also a simple mould will last longer because there are fewer moving parts. Then we could determine the material cost based on the volume of the chair and how many litres of material flow into the mould.

Finally, there's the production cycle. With this chair, it takes 16 seconds from the moment the first drop of plastic is injected into the mould until the time the chair closes up, which is really fast. At that point the mould and the material are still hot. Then you close the valves so the material gets stuck in there and then you want to cool it down as fast as you can to harden it. When it reaches a certain temperature you can open the mould and take the chair out.

So, although injection takes 16 seconds, the whole chair takes three or four minutes. Say you are producing eight hours a day, you know how many chairs you can do a day. For the whole cost of the chair, you work out how much it costs to run the machine for a day, divide by the number of chairs you can produce during that time and add the material cost.

The price of the chair also includes the investment. Usually companies try to pay off the investment of the tool within the first three years. Say the tool costs 100,000 euros and in the first three years you expect to sell 100,000 chairs, with every single chair you add another euro to the cycle cost to pay off the tool. Which means after three years you can either bring the price down by one euro or earn the euro.

I'm a designer, not a business person, but I'm learning about this, as far as it has an effect on my work as a designer. The more information I have about such things, the easier it is to make decisions in the design process.

You made a few chairs first for the plastics fair.

This wasn't strategy or choice. BASF wanted to promote the material at the big international plastics fair [the K Trade Fair] which takes place in Düsseldorf every three years. The first meeting we had with BASF was in June 2006 and the plastics fair was in October 2007. We just made it with that first production run. Then, after the fair we had another five months or so until the real market launch of the chair during the Milan Furniture Fair in April 2008. That gave us time to rework the tool and make some adjustments.

What were you refining at that time?

To be honest, we refined quite a lot of things! The first generation of chairs had some structural problems and we built up material, creating a beam in front of the seat. The crucial section is between the seat and the leg, so we made structural changes there, which also helped with the mould-flow. Also we cut a part out of the middle of the chair and made it slimmer.

> *How hard is it to make these changes? Presumably you have to change the mould.*

It's hard. Of course you try to avoid this as much as possible because it is an extra cost, but in a project of this kind of complexity and ambition you always know you can't get it right first time. BASF told us that for every single piece of plastic they mould in the car industry they probably make three generations of mould before they get it right.

What I like about designing for industry is that it's really a development process. In the end you want to press the button and these things fall off the machine – seeing a quantity of the same thing is a very great sensation. Because the process is so rationalized, you need time to think things through so all the problems are solved – it's not like making a one-off. I really like this length of thinking time because it allows for mistakes, trial and error, a learning curve, which means you can go deeper and deeper into the project.

We wanted to produce a chair for public spaces, which meant it would have to pass certain strict tests. You know what the requirements are and you can feed them into the computer and simulate how the chair will behave. The test facility we use is an Italian one, which is very good. After we ran the simulations everything seemed fine, and then when we got the chairs out of that first production run we sat on them and they felt all wrong. And the reason why that happened is very interesting. Something none of us had thought about it. Why it failed was because the tests are based on a four-legged chair, not on a cantilever chair. The behaviour of a cantilever chair is so different. You can imagine what kind of sideways movement you might have from the back part swinging and creating a lateral force on the chair, which you don't have on a four-legged chair. And of course the test doesn't test for that because four-legged chairs don't do that.

So the chairs were moving sideways?

We wanted a certain spring in the cantilever when you move backwards. The first chairs performed pretty much as we expected in that way. But what we hadn't taken into account was this sideways movement. The Panton chair, which is a plastic cantilever, is rock solid, so it couldn't provide a reference. To write the programme for the computer simulation, we took a cantilever tubular steel chair that felt right and we put that in the testing rig. Then we performed all the required tests – so many kilos on the seat and back and so on – and recorded how far the seat went down. And we said that if the seat of the steel chair goes down by 40 millimetres, that's what we need to get to.

When we put our plastic chair into the same simulation, we could see that it would only go down by 20 millimetres, which meant we had to make it softer. We could achieve this by making a section thinner, so that the leg, for example, becomes more flexible. With a wooden chair, I'd take a plane and plane some material off. With plastic you have another lever – you can change the chemical formula to make the material softer. On the computer they can very easily simulate the softer material ingredient and experiment until the seat goes down by 40 millimetres. Really, this was a new experience for me, where you pare off a millimetre here or there, and we could do this either by changing the geometry or by changing the chemistry, something invisible.

What happened after the chair was launched?

It's been in production ever since. There were still a few things to adjust. We had a problem with the colours, which again was something we didn't really think about. Choosing the colours is like giving a name to a product – you think, what colours would this thing look good in? I thought you could do plastics in any colour because all you do is add pigment. But the plastic has to be injected at 120 degrees, and at that high temperature the pigments for the red and the orange began to burn. So we would get little black dots on the surface and we didn't know what they were, until the BSAF people found out that it was actually pigment burning. Because we can't reduce the temperature, we had to find another pigment of the same colour that would be less sensitive to the heat and that took half a year and a lot of testing. Crazy stuff, a little, little detail like that. So for most of last year, Plank were only able to deliver black, white, grey and blue.

Another issue has to do with stacking. We designed the chair so that the higher you stack the more it goes back into a vertical tower. But when we made the structural changes to the front part, the geometry changed slightly, the chair became more front-heavy and we don't get this backward movement anymore. In practice, you stack three and the fourth becomes a bit of problem. That's something we haven't solved yet. We put little rubber buffers at the points of contact, so the chairs don't damage each other when they stack. Now we've designed a little plastic clip – you stack four and then you put the clip on and it holds them together.

Because we were part of the whole development, because of the difficult start and all the failures, we still have so much respect for this chair. When we showed it at the fair – and this always happens when you show it in public – people took it for granted and they sat on it as if it was the most natural, obvious thing to do, that it would hold. And that's very nice.

Left: The form of the Myto emerged through a process of hand modelling, with dimensions taken from the model and input into the computer to translate the geometry into 3D data.

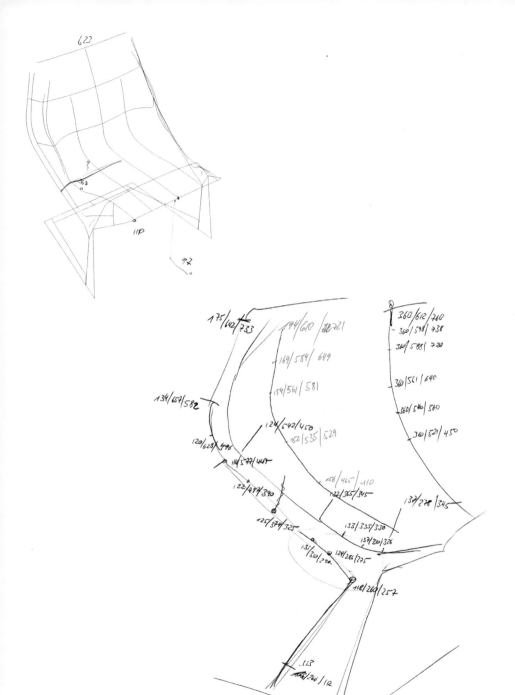

Left: Lightweight aluminium mesh – responsive, cheap and easy to work – was chosen as the material for modelling the form of the chair. The black tape indicates the supporting framework on the mesh. At an early stage it became clear that the interplay between a solid frame and a perforated surface would be the basis of the chair's design.

Right: The Myto is the world's first plastic cantilever chair that actually performs as a cantilever – in other words, is capable of movement.

Below: Red tape was applied to the fragile model in order to translate its geometry into 3D computer data.

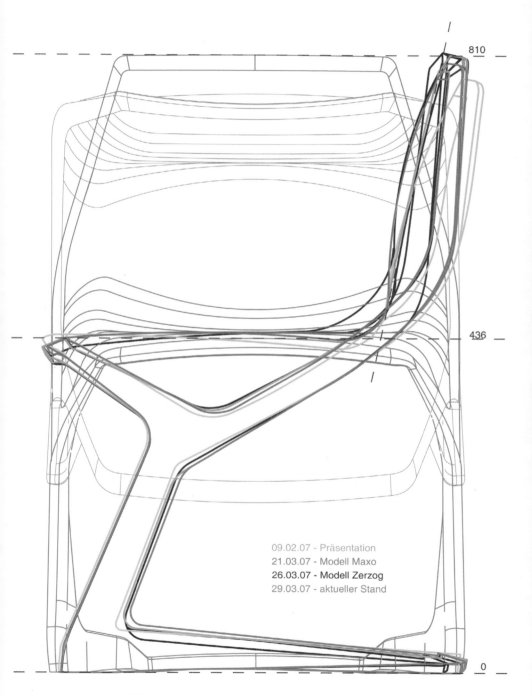

810

436

0

09.02.07 - Präsentation
21.03.07 - Modell Maxo
26.03.07 - Modell Zerzog
29.03.07 - aktueller Stand

Left above: Applying red tape to the model. Paper and cardboard were used during the modelling as well as metal mesh.

Left centre and below: Various permutations for the seat structure were investigated using adhesive tape and markers.

Right above and centre: Early ideas for the seat structure included asymmetrical lines and wicker-like patterning. These were tried out on 1:1 print-outs.

Right below: Konstantin Grcic working on the final grid of the seat structure, which was ultimately determined by the flow characteristics of the plastic material and the movement of the tool.

While early 'sketches' or models were produced using aluminium mesh, further models in polystyrene foam enabled the seating comfort of the chair to be assessed. At a later stage, the design was prototyped using selective laser sintering technology (SLS), which reproduced the precise 3D geometry of the computer data. This model could then be worked on in the studio to make adjustments.

The fast exchange of 3D computer data between the three project partners – plastics manufacturer, designer and furniture company – was essential to the success of the project, speeding up the process by enabling the simultaneous development of engineering and design.

At each phase of the design, the computer was able to analyse every aspect of performance, from stacking to the effect of dynamic and static stress. Additionally, mould-flow simulations and material testing allowed the engineering team to adjust the properties of the plastic material.

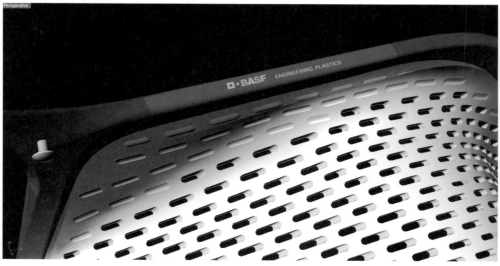

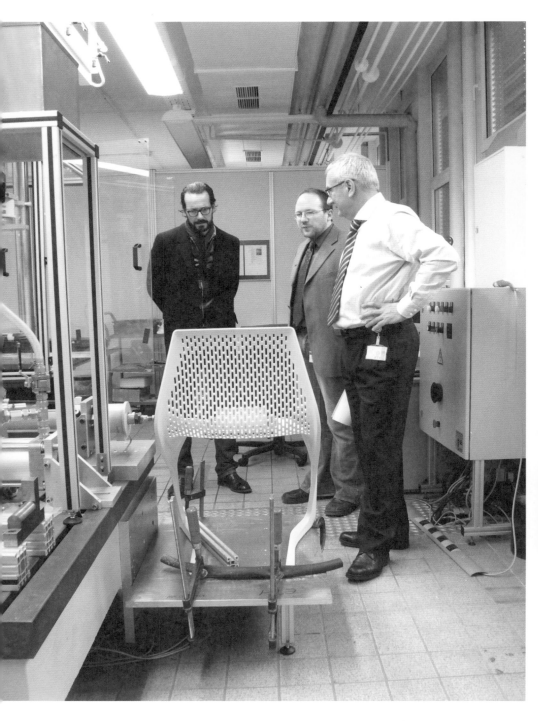

Left: The first off-tool chairs were tested in the BASF laboratories in Ludwigshafen.

Right: At the production site in Italy, the first off-tool chair is loaded with bags of the newly developed grade of Ultradur® High Speed. Throughout the design process, changes could be made either by altering the geometry of the design – for example making a section thicker or thinner – or by altering the chemical formula of the material.

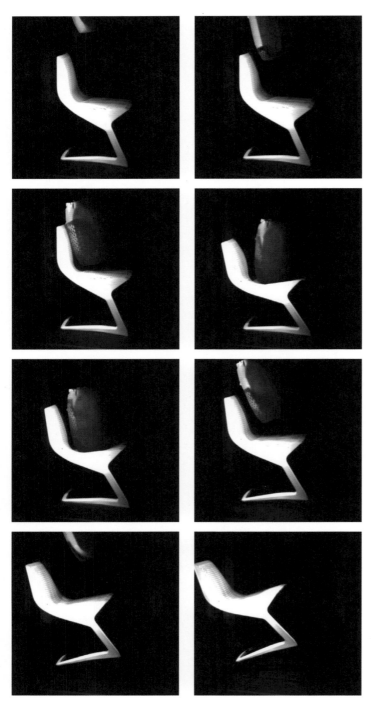

Left: At the BASF laboratories, the Myto was subjected to a series of tests. In this case the chair withstood a heavy load dropping from a height of 3 metres.

Right above: In the some of the early attempts, the plastic material failed to close in the seat. Part of the development process was to make changes that would shift the area of closure up to the backrest, which is a less structurally important part of the chair. This was achieved by making the seat taper, so there was a thicker section of mesh towards the front, giving the material an easier entry to the mould.

Right below: A chair designed for use in public spaces must pass a series of strict tests.

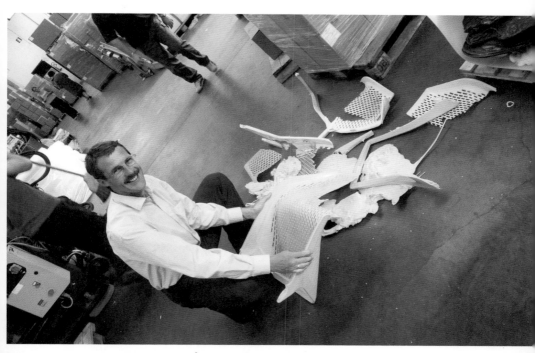

The mould, or tool, is a huge steel block that comes in two parts, engineered into the positive and negative forms of the chair. Inside are complex heating and cooling chambers. Before the plastic material is injected into it, the mould is heated so that the plastic will flow. The plastic is injected at three points at the front of the chair.

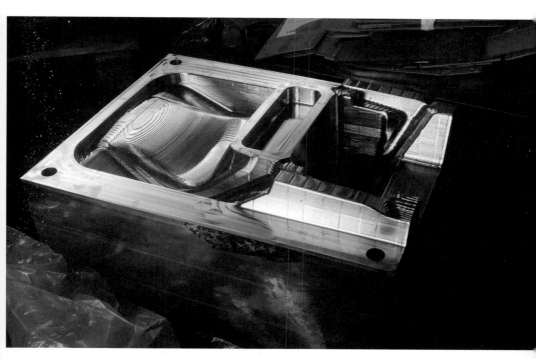

Left: Subtle corrections were made to the frame of the chair in the later stages of development.

Right above: Handwritten markings by the production engineer specified the different material compositions tested by the plastics manufacturer BASF.

Right centre: Konstantin Grcic, Martin Plank, Biagio Cisotti and Michael Plank discussing final details.

Right below: The chair is available in a number of bright colours. Achieving the right red and orange shades proved difficult because the pigments began to burn when the plastic was heated to the high temperature required for injection into the mould.

The Myto was launched in October 2007 at the K Trade Fair, the world's biggest plastics fair, held in Düsseldorf. Only 11 months had elapsed from the first meeting between BASF and the designer to the chair's premiere. It has been in production ever since.

Selected works

Designer:
Konstantin Grcic

Mayday, 1999
Portable lamp
Producer: Flos

The Mayday lamp was
designed to be a tool for
use in many different
situations. The on/off switch
is incorporated into
the handle and there are
two spikes to wind up the
5m-long cable, as well as a
hook on the end to hang up
the light. The white funnel is
both reflector and protector
of the light source. The
smooth polypropylene
plastic gives off a warm
and diffused light and is
strong enough to withstand
accidental knocks.

Chair_ONE, 2004
Producer: Magis

Chair_ONE is constructed
like a football, with a number
of flat planes assembled at
angles to each other to create
the three-dimensional form.
It received enormous public
attention when it was
launched. The angular
faceted seat is made of
die-cast aluminium.

Miura, 2005
Bar stool
Producer: Plank

This monoblock plastic
bar stool arose out of a
commission from the Italian
furniture company Plank.
The design of the stool is
strongly based on principles
of construction, although
the shape was conceived by
working in a more sculptural
manner. The complex free-
form surfaces were designed
on the computer.

Index

Glossary

Arts and Crafts movement
Movement pioneered by William Morris that sought to reconnect architecture and design with traditional (that is, pre-industrial) crafts, materials and values.

bentwood Wood used in furniture-making that has been shaped mechanically, often using steam.

bergère ('shepherdess') A deep-seated upholstered armchair popular in eighteenth-century France.

cabinetmaker A highly skilled turner or carpenter who makes high-quality furniture.

cabriole leg An S-shaped leg used in ancient China and Greece and adopted in European furniture styles in the early eighteenth century. A notable characteristic of Chippendale chairs.

cantilever chair A chair design with no back legs but which relies on the properties of its constituent materials to support the sitter.

chaise longue (French: 'long chair') A chair with a seat long enough to support the legs. A furniture type popular in eighteenth-century France, derived from classical precedents. Also sometimes known as a 'chaise lounge' in North America, owing to a misunderstanding of 'longue'.

chamfer A sloping cut-away edge where two (wooden) surfaces meet.

classicism A style of architecture developed during the Renaissance that looked back to the cultural achievements of ancient Greece and Rome and that privileged the ideas of proportion, symmetry and order. In the eighteenth century the style was vigorously revived and later became known as neoclassicism.

De Stijl An early twentieth-century Dutch movement in art, design and architecture that married the modernist tenets of harmony and order with a concern with the spiritual.

fauteuil (French: 'armchair') A wooden open-armed chair, with upholstered back and seat; a popular eighteenth-century French furniture type.

hardwood The wood from a broadleaved tree such as oak or beech, not necessarily harder than softwood.

klismos An classical Greek chair type with a curved backrest and sweeping sabre legs, widely adopted in the neoclassical revival of the eighteenth century.

love seat A two-seater sofa, often designed in an S-shape that enables the sitters to face one another.

modernism A twentieth-century movement in art, design and architecture that sought a radical break from historical styles and that privileged functionalism, simplicity and modern materials.

neoclassicism *See* classicism.

sabre leg A curved sweeping leg, like a sabre.

selective laser sintering (SLS) Manufacturing technique that uses a high-power laser to convert digital data or scans into a three-dimensional object, usually using particles of plastic, glass, ceramic or metal. Widely used in the creation of prototypes.

softwood Wood from coniferous trees such as pine.

splat The central vertical element of the chair back, often carved and a key element in identifying a cabinetmaker's style.

turner Someone skilled at turning wood on a lathe; a carpenter or furniture-maker.

veneer A thin layer of decorative wood used to cover a coarser wood or other material forming the main frame of an item of furniture.

wing chair A chair with a high backrest and high, enclosing armrests, or 'wings'.

Picture Credits

Credits

First published in 2010
by Conran Octopus Ltd
in association with
The Design Museum

Conran Octopus,
a part of Octopus Publishing
Group, Endeavour House,
189 Shaftesbury Avenue,
London WC2H 8JY
www.octopusbooks.co.uk

A Hachette UK Company
www.hachette.co.uk

Distributed in the United
States and Canada by
Hachette Book Group USA,
237 Park Avenue, New York,
NY 10017 USA

British Library Cataloguing-
in-Publication Data.
A catalogue record for
this book is available
from the British Library.

Text written by:
Elizabeth Wilhide

Publisher:
Lorraine Dickey
Consultant Editor:
Deyan Sudjic
Managing Editor:
Sybella Marlow
Editor:
Robert Anderson

Art Director:
Jonathan Christie
Design:
Untitled
Picture Researcher:
Anne-Marie Hoines

Production Manager:
Katherine Hockley

ISBN: 978 1 84091 546 4
Printed in China